UNDER THE SEA

First published in Canada by Whitecap Books
351 Lynn Avenue, North Vancouver, British Columbia, V7J 2C4

First published in 2001
Text and illustrations copyright © Random House Australia
Pty Ltd, 2001

ISBN: 1-55285-195-8

Children's Publisher: Linsay Knight
Series Editor: Marie-Louise Taylor
Managing Editor: Marie-Louise Taylor
Art Director: Linda Maxwell
Design concept: Stan Lamond
Production Manager: Linda Watchorn
Publishing Co-ordinator: Pia Gerard

Illustrator: Garry Fleming; assisted by Andrew Patsalou and Spike
Wademan
Consultant: Reg Lipson
Writer: Reg Lipson
Educational Consultant: Pamela Hook

Film separation by Pica Colour Separation Overseas Pte Ltd,
Singapore
Printed in Hong Kong by Sing Cheong Printing Co. Ltd.

When you see a word in **bold** type, you'll find its
meaning in the Glossary at the back of the book.

Get a FREE POSTER!
Go to page 63 for details.

UNDER THE SEA

Consultant **Reg Lipson**
Illustrator **Garry Fleming**

WHITECAP
BOOKS

CONTENTS

CONTENTS

Deep sea stories

Do you look forward to a fun day of surf and sand? All those waves to catch and rock pools to explore. Did you know that Earth is the only planet in our Solar System to have oceans? We are lucky!

THE ANCIENT OCEAN

The oceans have been in existence for a very long time, almost as long as the planet itself. Now they cover just over two-thirds of the Earth's surface, and are up to 11.5 kilometres (7 miles) deep. Oceans are composed of salt water and vary in temperature from below freezing point to very hot.

PEOPLE AND THE OCEAN

Human history has always been linked with the sea because many of us live near coasts. Throughout time the oceans have provided us with transport, food and adventure. Well hidden below the surface, often choppy and rough, you'll find billions of nature's weirdest creations. Strange plants and animals live together, not always in peace but sometimes fighting to the death for territory and food. For humans, the oceans can be dangerous. However, if we respect the ocean, we can enjoy swimming, sailing, fishing, surfing and diving.

In days gone by, people imagined that all sorts of frightening creatures lived in the sea.

Wet and wild

How would you like to go swimming with one of these creatures? I don't think so!

GIANT REPTILES OF THE SEA

During the time of the great land **dinosaurs**, around 200 to 100 million years ago, their cousins, the marine **reptiles**, were kings of the seas, and so far as we know not even one dinosaur successfully lived in the seas. Many marine reptiles reached huge sizes: 10–15 metres (33–49 feet) long. They were among the largest and most savage creatures of all time, even more savage than any monster ever dreamt up for a horror movie! Now, sadly (perhaps) all but a very few of these ancient monsters have become extinct. We only have crocodiles, turtles and marine **iguanas** to remind us of the time of the great sea reptiles.

mosasaur

Ancient turtles grew to 5 metres (16 feet) and fed on all sorts of things. This one has grabbed a 9 metre (30 foot) long squid.

The ancient sea crocodiles were true marine reptiles and, unlike their sluggish land cousins we see today, they were agile, swift hunters. Some even swallowed stones, holding them in their stomachs to help digest some of the hard-shelled critters they ate.

Archaeopteryx

Tanystropheus

Tanystropheus was a curious looking marine reptile, with a neck 3–4 metres (10–13 feet) long that it could wave around to capture fish or a careless flying **Archaeopteryx**!

LOOK AGAIN!

The Loch Ness monster may be a plesiosaur that survived the dinosaur extinction.

mosasaur

Mosasaurs varied in size between 2 and 14 metres (7 and 46 feet) and ate other reptiles, fish and giant squid. Although the plesiosaurs were extremely successful marine reptiles, this one wasn't so lucky.

plesiosaur

A wall of waves

Imagine playing on the sand on a warm, windless afternoon. Sounds perfect! But somewhere, way out in the ocean, there is a small wave of energy 'flying' through the water towards you. Little waves like this one are quite fearsome, and have caused more destruction and death than any creature that has ever lived.

Scientists have set up an early warning system in the Pacific Ocean region to detect and warn of tsunamis.

A KILLER WAVE

If an undersea earthquake moves rocks on the seabed it can start waves of energy (just like the one you cause when you drop a pebble into a pool). These ocean waves, called **tsunamis**, may be over 100 kilometres (62 miles) long, have enormous energy and travel through the ocean at incredible speeds. Out at sea, tsunamis are small, but as they move into shallower waters near coasts, they can reach around 40 metres (130 feet) high. Imagine a wall of water as high as a fifteen-storey building rushing towards you and your home. There is little chance of escaping. Tsunamis have caused thousands of deaths, and terrible destruction of villages and towns.

Tsunamis are also called 'seismic sea waves' or 'tidal waves'. Tidal wave is not a good name because tides have nothing to do with tsunamis.

Treasure!

Gold and silver bullion, gem-encrusted weapons, ornate jewellery, pieces of eight—who hasn't dreamed of treasure? There's much still to be found deep in the sea. Amazingly, very few of all the Spanish 'treasure ships' that sailed from South America to Asia ever reached their destination. Each ship carried about 80 tonnes of gold and silver, so imagine the wealth lying on the ocean floor!

These days, the historical value of shipwrecks is well known, and there are laws protecting wrecks from pillaging by greedy or dishonest divers.

Time capsules

Not all treasure is gold, silver or jewels. Shipwrecks are time capsules, full of clues about the past. Fragments of clothing, furniture, eating utensils, tools, weapons, books—things used in days gone by—still exist somewhere beneath the sea. We just have to find them!

EASY MONEY?

Despite the dangers of the deep and tales of sea monsters, people dived into the frightening depths to find these lost treasures. They still dive today. Nowadays, scholars study ancient manuscripts and books for clues as to where treasure ships may lie before the first dive takes place. But even with the best information and using modern undersea technology, the chances of success are small, because the sea does not give up its secrets easily.

Taking too much

When many people think about the sea, they think of storms, hurricanes, shipwrecks, sharks and other dangers of the deep. But in spite of its reputation as a killer, the sea has always provided us with a rich bounty.

CURTAINS OF DEATH

From the earliest times, people have found food simply by walking along the beach and collecting the creatures of the **intertidal** zone, like limpets, snails and seaweed. Later, spears, hooks and lines, and nets were used to catch fish. Unfortunately, however, people became greedy. Fishing fleets became equipped with long nets stretching across the sea for hundreds of kilometres. Sadly, these have also become 'curtains of death'. They catch not only fish, but also sharks, stingrays, dolphins, porpoises, seals and turtles. Once entangled in the strong fibre, these animals die. Successful fishing has come at a cost. The numbers of many species have dwindled and are still reducing. Fortunately, regulations now outlaw certain fishing techniques and fishing at those times of the year when fish are reproducing. This gives fish populations a chance to recover.

About 80 million tonnes of fish are sold each year in the Tokyo fish market!

Collecting food from the intertidal zone.

Move it!

The sea has not only provided food for us, it has also opened up the world. Many thousands of years ago the only way of getting around was by walking. It wasn't long before clever people began to make rafts, so they could explore not only what was in the sea, but also what lay beyond it. The sea was our first highway!

NEW FRONTIERS

As populations increased and areas became crowded, it is not surprising that disputes occurred over land and fishing territories. Thoughts of new lands, new food sources and new places for homes inspired some brave souls to pack their belongings and as much food and fresh water as they could store, and head off across the unknown sea. Can you imagine packing your goodies onto a raft made of wood and straw lashed together with primitive rope? Many perished, but the rewards for those who found new lands were immense—new land to garden, new animals to farm, and plenty of space for all.

Some journeys made by our ancestors were truly amazing. There is evidence suggesting that they may have crossed the entire Pacific Ocean—an incredible distance of over 7,500 kilometres (4,600 miles)!

LOOK AGAIN!

Travellers used their knowledge of the stars to guide them across the sea at night.

AN AMAZING WONDERLAND

There is a huge variety of creatures found in our oceans. Sea stars crawl over the sandy bottom, feeding on seaweed and **detritus**. A sea star may bring its stomach out of its mouth, and digest its food outside its body! Bristle worms are deadly hunters, equipped with massively strong jaws. Once a small creature is in its grip, it won't get away. Stingrays rest with most of their body buried— only their eyes are above the sand watching for predators. Heart urchins extend their tube feet from their burrows to feed on food lying on the sand surface.

LOOK AGAIN!

We know the sea star has died because it is upside down and we can see its grooves.

Flounders can change their body colour to keep hidden from both prey and predators.

stingray

sea star (starfish or asteroid)

bristleworm

Bivalves (pipis and cockles) live hidden just beneath the sand surface.

Sandhoppers live beneath the sand and quickly eat any dead seaweed and animal bodies. Without them our beaches would be very dirty and smelly!

Sand in your shoes

When you look at a sandy sea bottom or beach, you may not see much—some seaweed, shells, a crab. But remember that the sea is a savage place to be, so many creatures bury themselves for protection or are coloured to match the sand. They play a deadly game of hide and seek. Being discovered may mean becoming someone else's breakfast!

Many crabs bury themselves with just their eyes protruding above the sand. Others roam around, fairly safe in their armour-plated bodies, looking for food.

crab

heart urchin

The moon snail creeps along the sand hunting for bivalves. Its round, rough tongue uses chemicals to drill right through the shell. It then sucks out the digested guts of its prey. You may have seen bivalve shells, with a neat hole drilled right through them, scattered on the beach.

Some sea cucumbers live beneath the sand, taking mouthfuls of sand and digesting any living (or dead) thing from it. The sand passes through the cucumber's body and out as waste. Have you ever tasted a sand sandwich?

Just a drop!

Just above the water's edge is a special strip of the Earth's surface. This narrow band (intertidal zone) is not always land nor always sea, but is wet or dry according to the tides. The plants and animals that live here are very tough.

MASTER SURVIVORS

These plants and animals survive a huge range of temperatures—from blazing summer heat to icy, drying, mid-winter winds, and even flooding by freshwater after heavy rain. At the very top of this zone, well above the sea, are the creatures and plants that don't need to be wet, they only need some sea mist (moisture) to survive. As long as their gills are moist, they are able to get the oxygen they need to live. If you look closely, you will see how each creature or plant keeps itself moist.

Limpets move around on a large muscular foot, and use their very tough, rough tongue to scrape tiny plants from the rock surface. To keep water under the shell after the tide has receded, they produce a sticky mucus that acts as a watertight seal.

lichen

If you move a chiton or limpet, notice the wet spot beneath. This is their water reservoir. Make sure you put them back just beneath the water so they can regain their moisture.

LOOK
AGAIN!

Chitons have a flexible covering made up of eight overlapping plates.

sea snail

limpets

sea snail

Chitons eat algae. They can hang onto surfaces that aren't flat and still form a watertight seal around their edge.

chitons

No sandals!

The middle intertidal zone, or rock pool zone, is the home of animals and plants that need more than just a spray, but don't need to be wet all the time. Fishes, algae, sea slugs, snails and anemones live in rock pools—all hunting or being hunted.

SAFETY FIRST, LAST AND ALWAYS

When exploring a rock pool, always wear shoes that can be fastened with laces and that have a strong, flexible, non-slip sole. Never wear sandals or thongs! It's a good idea to wear at least one rubber glove for protection against cuts, stings or bites. Use this hand to feel around with. Remember that many of these animals are well armed, and camouflaged so they are difficult to see.

DON'T TOUCH!

The blue-ringed **octopod** is found in rock pools of South Pacific beaches. It has no bones, so can squeeze through tiny spaces looking for crabs to eat. It can also change the colour and roughness of its skin to match its surroundings, so remains almost invisible to both **prey** and **predator**. Only when disturbed does it display its electric-blue rings. If touched, it can deliver a nip with its beak, or a lick with its roughened tongue. Deadly venom then oozes from its mouth into these tiny injuries.

sea snail

fish

WARNING!

Never touch a blue-ringed octopod or place your unprotected hand into a rock pool!

chiton

mussels

barnacles

sea cucumber

algae

sea anemone

When investigating the intertidal zone always face towards the water. Even when bending down, make sure you're facing the sea, so you'll be able to see big waves and avoid getting hurt.

crab

sea centipede

BLUE-RINGED OCTOPOD

Hangin' on for dear life

Below the rock pool zone live the 'toughest of the tough'— perhaps the toughest plants and animals on this planet.

DON'T LET GO!

Imagine living where you are constantly pounded, bashed and smashed by the thundering, crashing waves. It's hard to believe anything could survive such a battering and yet when one looks, there are plenty of plants and animals. They need a really good glue (like the barnacles and tube worms have), or maybe strong bristles that grow into the rocks (like the mussels have), to hang on with and withstand the force of the waves. The crabs that live here have very strong muscles in their legs and pointed feet with which to hang on. Pick up one of these long-legged crabs at your own risk! As well as being able to hang on, of course, you need a very tough body or home to withstand the force of the crashing waves. Otherwise you have to be as good as the crabs at seeking shelter in cracks and crevices.

The plants that live in this zone are tough too. Pick up a piece of kelp (seaweed) and try and break it, tear it or pull it apart. Why are the biggest kelps in such a tough place? Because they need the plentiful oxygen found in the swirling, crashing, well-aerated waves.

kelp

mussels

periwinkles

tube
worms

barnacles

starfish

limpets

LOOK
AGAIN!
Barnacles and limpets have
hard, flattish, sloping
shells so water runs
over them.

sea urchins

red bait crab

25

Under we go

Imagine how people felt hundreds of years ago when they learned about the tonnes of sunken treasure and the variety of fish hidden beneath the waves. Many people were terrified by stories of huge sharks, giant gropers and other monsters of the deep. So the first divers were considered to be very courageous indeed.

Although we know there are 'monsters' in the sea, most of them are much too small, or live too deep, to worry us. The worst monsters are those we dream up ourselves.

Early, hard-hat divers wore a diving suit that included a large helmet made of metal.

Modern day divers wear light and manageable equipment.

FIGHTING MONSTERS

Mistakenly, early divers believed that oceans would only be a safe place for humans if as many sharks as possible were killed, and so they invented weapons such as the 'powerhead'. This single shot weapon was aimed at the shark's backbone just behind the head, and caused immediate death. Nowadays, we know that most sharks certainly aren't human-eaters. In fact, most don't take much notice of us at all, so the seas have become a wonderful playground full of adventure.

LOOK
AGAIN!
Air was pumped to the hard-hat diver through a pipe from a boat above him.

Underwater delights

How would you like to explore the weightless, beautiful and silent world of the oceans? All you need to do is learn to use self-contained underwater breathing apparatus (scuba).

AN AMAZING SHOW

How would you feel swimming through schools of rainbow coloured fish, near a 3 metre (10 foot) shark, alongside a huge turtle, having a venomous sea snake swim up and flick its tongue all over your face mask or being looked over by a 5 metre (16 foot) wide manta ray? Sounds frightening but these things happen to divers every day! And none of these creatures seem to mind too much. After all, the seas are their home, they're much more suited to it than us, and so if they do get worried they just move off— usually much too fast for us to follow.

reef shark

coral trout

manta ray

LOOK AGAIN!
The colours of the corals come from living polyps. Dead coral is white.

many-lined sweetlips

anenome fish

turtle

sea snake

The crown-of-thorns starfish is covered with long, poisonous spines.

Death by injection

One fish paralysed by a single tentacle and the other safe! What's going on here?

TOUCH AT YOUR OWN PERIL!

Jellyfish and sea anemones belong to a group of creatures known as the **cnidarians** (say nii-DARE-ee-ans). They have stinging tentacles around their mouth, and most are lethal killers to small marine animals! All over the surface of each tentacle there are many little capsules containing **nematocysts**. These barbed, poisoned harpoons are coiled inside the capsule waiting for some poor fish or shrimp to make contact with the bristle-like trigger. Then POW!—the capsule flies open, the harpoon shoots out and the victim is impaled. As it struggles, more and more nematocysts are fired, more venom is injected until the victim is paralysed—or dead! Then the tentacles retract and the prey is taken into the mouth and digested.

anenome fish or clownfish

LOOK
AGAIN!

It can take only
one jellyfish tentacle
to paralyse and kill
a fish.

A fish is caught by a
jellyfish. Sometimes,
just swimming close
to a jellyfish tentacle will
cause enough 'chemical'
contact to fire nematocysts.

NEMATOCYST   NEMATOCYST
COILED READY   'FIRED'
FOR ACTION

How does the anemone fish (left) live within the stinging
tentacles of sea anemones? This remarkable fish 'snuggles'
around underneath the anemone and coats its outer body
with the same slime or mucus used to prevent the tentacles
from firing on contact with each other. The anemone thinks
the fish is part of its own body!

31

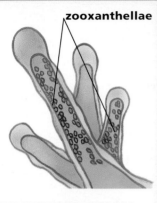

zooxanthellae

THE FLESHY BODY TUBE OF A CORAL POLYP

Unlike our homes, coral polyps' homes are enormous in size—the only living thing that can be seen from outer space!

INVESTIGATE

Builders extraordinaire

The enormous size of coral reefs is perhaps only fully appreciated by those lucky enough to dive among them. It's like swimming through a city of skyscrapers—you can't see the bottom and sometimes you can't see the top, and you are surrounded by massive underwater 'buildings'.

CONSTRUCTING A HOME

Most remarkable of all, these mountains are built by small animals and plants working together. Billions of miniature coral animals called **polyps** live alongside each other and secrete limestone in, and around, their bodies. Thus they build their homes. Yet, these coral animals are only able to produce large amounts of **limestone** when their bodies contain small plants (**zooxanthellae**). The plants live inside the body of the coral polyp, using its waste products to produce food for themselves, as well as for the polyp. This is a pretty good partnership!

In forests, some animals hide between the plants. In coral reefs, some plants hide within the bodies of the animals!

Unbelievable!

To dive in underwater forests among the towering kelps (the longest plants in the world), to search the colourful and ever-changing sea bottom and boulders, is to be constantly surprised.

COLOUR AND MOVEMENT

While the beauty and biodiversity of coral 'cities' is universally accepted, it is a fact that colder seas contain more animals and larger algae species than tropical seas. As you swim under the sea, everywhere there are creatures—sea stars, urchins, brilliantly coloured gorgonian fans, and the ever-present fishes. Then suddenly, out of nowhere, a face peers straight into your mask and gives you a fright!

And what about seals, the superb acrobats of the seas? They flash past, turn, twist, somersault, flip back on themselves and playfully nip at a diver's equipment. Seals really are the puppies of the underwater world.

LOOK
AGAIN!
Kelps are the longest sea plants, yet their fronds never fall to the ocean bottom.

Freezing!

Almost all living things need oxygen, and the maximum number of plants and animals that can live in any expanse of water depends on how much oxygen that water contains.

TEEMING WITH LIFE

The more oxygen, the greater the number of living things that can survive. And did you know that the colder the water, the more oxygen it can hold? Antarctic waters are about -2° Celsius (28°Farenheit) and so it's no real surprise that they're full of living things. From tiny microscopic plants and animals right up through the food chain to the fishes, squids, penguins, leopard seals, sharks and the giant whales.

What an extraordinary creature the penguin is! No wonder early explorers had trouble deciding if it was a bird or not. Shaped like a fish, unable to fly in air but shoots through the water at about 20 kilometres (12 miles) per hour, doesn't appear to have feathers but keeps warm with a thick layer of fat beneath its skin—this is a bird? Yes, it is.

Leopard seals usually live alone and are savage predators—one of the few smart enough, and fast enough, to prey on young seals and penguins. With their fearsome jaws they can flick their victims into the air with such force that the skin is ripped off.

Sea spiders (called 'pycnogonid') vary in size from a few millimetres to 1 metre (3 feet) across, but they're not dangerous to humans. They live in all cold, deep seas (tropical, temperate and polar) and have been found in the intertidal zone down to 7 kilometres (4 miles) deep.

Open spaces

Within the oceans of this planet there are many habitats—sandy bottoms, sandy beaches, rocky reefs of the temperate seas, tropical coral reefs. But none is more interesting than the open spaces of the vast oceans.

flying fish

sargassum weed

sargassum fish

crab

It is quite remarkable to discover that these seaweed cities do not sink as most seaweeds do, and so these communities live and thrive.

THE GREAT OUT THERE!

In the open ocean, some fishes fly and schools of tuna move at speeds of up to 80 kilometres (50 miles) an hour! Many kilometres offshore, in a sprawling section of the open Atlantic Ocean, is the Sargasso Sea. Here creatures live among the sprawling golden and brown tendrils of sargassum weed, hunting, feeding and avoiding being eaten themselves, so that they can reproduce at every opportunity. There is only one hope for survival—their camouflage must be perfect and their bodies unmoving. Or sometimes they are **toxic** or poisonous and brightly coloured—this is a clear announcement to predators of their unpleasant taste.

Portuguese man o' war

Portuguese men o' war sail across the oceans injecting deathly venom into anything unfortunate enough to touch their long trailing tentacles.

LOOK AGAiN!

How many animals can you see camouflaged in the brown sargassum weed?

tuna

Can you think why there is more plankton in cold waters than in warm waters?

sunfish

Tropical waters have fewer plankton, so are clearer and bluer than temperate and cold seas.

jellyfish

Most plankton are tiny, but there are some outstanding exceptions. Jellyfish and sunfish may be up to 3 metres (10 feet) long, and salps may grow to 10 metres (33 feet). Although they are large, they don't move efficiently, so are classified as plankton.

Wanderers

You can't see them, but millions of tonnes of tiny organisms, both plant and animal, live and thrive in the oceans. Each has its own name, yet they are all known by the general name of **plankton**. *Plankton is any living thing that swims feebly and moves mainly where the sea takes it.*

MAKING ENERGY

The amount of plankton affects the clarity and colour of sea water—the more plankton, the less clear the water and the greener it appears. Plankton also play an important role as food producers and gas exchangers within the ocean waters. It is within the tiny bodies of plant plankton (**phytoplankton**) living within metres of the ocean's surface, that most of the world's **photosynthesis** takes place. Photosynthesis is important for all life on Earth. During photosynthesis, energy from sunlight changes carbon dioxide gas and water into food sources for other creatures. Microscopic animal plankton (**zooplankton**) also swim near the ocean's surface. They might be fish larvae or tiny crustaceans.

salp

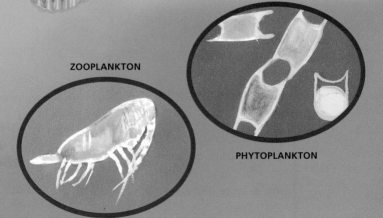

ZOOPLANKTON

PHYTOPLANKTON

Conquerors
of the water

*Although there are about 25,000 species of fishes (including sharks and rays) already studied by scientists, this is probably only about half the total number that exist! There are more types of fishes than any other **vertebrate** animal.*

FISHES EVERYWHERE

Fishes (including sharks and rays) have been around for about 500 million years. Humans have only existed for less than one million years. Fishes live in fresh and salt water. They vary in size from a few grams, to the monstrous whale shark, which is 15 metres (50 feet) long and weighs more than 20 tonnes. Fishes occupy waters from 5 kilometres (3 miles) above sea level to 11.5 kilometres (7 miles) below—a range greater than any other vertebrate. They eat everything from microscopic plankton to whales.

—— **moray eel**

The scorpion fish lurks hidden among sponges and corals, waiting to pounce on its prey of fish and crustaceans. It looks more like a rock or shell than a fish.

The shape of a fish's body allows it to move quickly and easily through the water.

great white shark

Sight is an important sense for capturing prey and avoiding predators. Bony fishes that are active in the daytime see colour, while nocturnal (active at night) fishes, sharks and rays see mainly black and white.

Sharks have a mirror-like reflecting layer in the back of the eyeball, so in dull light they can see quite clearly.

TERRIFIC TEETH

Fishes' teeth vary in form depending on what they eat, and while the slicing teeth of some sharks are impressive, the inward pointing teeth of bony fishes like eels are also intriguing. They tilt inwards and are shaped like daggers (for holding not cutting), and they often grow from the bony upper roof of the mouth—these are called **vomer** teeth—as well as around the edges like our own. What chance does a fish have of escaping from the deadly grip of a moray eel?

Fixed but fabulous

On land, it's usually simple to pick out animals from plants, but it's trickier under the sea. Objects that don't move often turn out to be animals, not plants. Sponges, lace corals, sea mats, sea anemones, tube worms, hard corals and soft corals are commonly mistaken for plants.

YOU WON'T EAT ME!

The seas are full of creatures on the lookout for something to eat. Those animals that have survived living out in the open for hundreds of millions of years are masters of defence. Sponges, for example, can't run and can't hide; they just sit there and yet almost nothing attacks them. Why? Sponges produce many toxic and unpalatable substances within their flesh and in the mucus that coats their surface. Woe betide the poor creature who takes a mouthful. It tastes horrible! Some sponges have more deadly weapons embedded in their flesh. These are **spicules**. They are barbed spheres made of limestone and even glass!

anemone

SPONGE
SPICULES

branch coral

Can you work out how hard corals, soft corals, bryozoans, sea anemones and tube worms protect themselves?

sponge chimneys

algae

anemone

What's in a name?

When is a lace coral not a coral? Almost always. Lace corals (bryozoans) are small creatures that build a hard limestone skeleton similar to hard corals. So lace coral and hard coral colonies look similar. The bryozoa (animals) themselves however have a much more complicated body structure than that of a hard coral. Be careful of common names!

Softies

The 'softies' (molluscs) have been in the oceans of this planet for around 600 million years. Today, there are about 100,000 different kinds in our seas, including shellfish (bivalves, pipis) and snails in their tough shells, colourful sea slugs, octopods, squids and cuttlefish. It's hard to believe they are actually alike.

SUPER SQUID!

One of the most fearsome molluscs ever to have existed is the giant squid, and it still swims in our oceans today. These creatures weigh around 300 kilograms (660 pounds) and grow to a length of about 20 metres (65 feet). They live in the cold waters of the ocean depths, because it's only at these very low temperatures that their blood can carry enough oxygen for their needs. Most of our knowledge of this incredible creature has come from carcasses washed onto shorelines, or in earlier days, taken from the bellies of sperm whales. Only a few giant squid have ever been seen by people who lived to tell the tale.

LOOK AGAIN!

The long torpedo shape of the squid's body allows it to swim very fast.

MASSIVE MOLLUSCS

Giant squid aren't the only huge molluscs. On 2 December 1896, the remains of an octopod were washed up on a Florida beach in the United States. It weighed about 6 tonnes and the stump of the one partly rotted tentacle was 10 metres (33 feet) long. No doubt there are more amazing creatures to be discovered in our oceans.

The name for molluscs comes from a Latin word *mollis* meaning soft. While it's true that their bodies are soft, many are protected by a hard shell.

Squids and cuttlefish apply an irresistible deathly grip on a fish, as each sucker is armed with a circular set of 'teeth'. Not even the mucus coating of fishes allows them to slip out of this nasty situation!

Busting out all over

*Did you know that **arthropods** are probably the most successful group of animals on this planet? Crabs, shrimps, lobsters, sea spiders, sand hoppers, insects and land spiders make up about 95 per cent of all the Earth's animals!*

A FIGHTING FORTRESS

One look at an arthropod's body plan shows why they are so successful. It's like a military tank! Brain, heart, stomach, and all the vital workings of an arthropod's body, are safely tucked away inside the skeleton, which is on the outside of the body (**exoskeleton**). Such animals grow by weakening the exoskeleton, using chemicals in the blood, and drinking lots of sea water. This makes them swell inside, which splits the encasing armour. The animal then walks its soft internal body backwards out through the split. A new stronghold soon grows, and the excess water leaves the animal's body. The body size then reduces inside the new exoskeleton. This wondrous process is called arthropod 'ecdysis' (say ec-DIE-sis).

LOOK
AGAIN!
The crab has two powerful pincer claws that look like pliers. It uses them to grip prey.

Not all crab skeletons you find on the beach are from dead crabs; some are cast-off exoskeletons of previous moults.

A crab moves backwards out of its old exoskeleton—part of the incredible process of ecdysis.

Reptiles meek
and terrible

Some 60 million years ago, dinosaurs ruled the land, and their terrifying cousins, the marine reptiles, dominated the seas. It is lucky for us that we didn't exist at the same time, because we'd have probably ended up as a tasty morsel for them.

Saltwater crocodiles are definitely not meek creatures. These savage predators, which grow to a massive 10 metres (33 feet) long, have eaten humans! It certainly pays for us to treat these animals with respect.

sea snake

marine turtle

SWIMMERS AND DIVERS

There are only a few marine reptiles left on Earth, but they are exciting creatures. Marine turtles may be gentle, but they are marathon swimmers. These turtles can cover 2,600 kilometres (1,600 miles). They mate at sea and lay their eggs on sandy shores. Not so meek are the snakes that make their homes in the warmer waters of the western Pacific and Indian Oceans. Sea snakes are all **venomous**, in fact they are the most venomous groups of snakes on the planet. Fortunately, they are not aggressive and their short fangs mean that very little venom is released. They can dive to 100 metres (330 feet), and can remain submerged for almost two hours. They hunt fish and small eels.

The marine iguana of the Galapagos Islands is the only lizard that searches for food and eats it underwater. It likes algae from rocks, but will also eat small fish. It drinks sea water.

marine
iguana

As deep as can be!

On the deep floor of the ocean lies the seabed. Here no light penetrates—it is forever midnight. People once thought that the deep ocean had no life and that the seabed was flat. We now know that the seabed has enormous mountain ranges, higher than those on land, chasms deeper than the Grand Canyon, steep-sided valleys and plains of gently rolling hills.

THE MYSTERIOUS DEPTHS

In some places, **superheated steam** and black 'smoke' rush through cracks in the Earth's crust and around **hydrothermal vents** (or **'smokers'**). Unusual creatures prowl around these vents, such as white crabs and other **crustaceans**, long tube worms and bivalve molluscs. Strange fishes inhabit the ocean's depths. They have few muscles and reduced skeletons and bodies, and elastic stomachs to digest their food. Humans have not been to these depths because we can't deal with the great water pressure. There may be human footsteps on the Moon, but there are none on the bottom of the oceans! Scientists use remote operated vehicles (ROVs) to take lights, cameras and artificial hands to see these ghostly places.

'smokers'

tube worms

A fascinating food chain operates at the ocean depths. Bacteria get energy from chemical reactions with the smoke. The bacteria are then eaten by other creatures.

Can you imagine a trench in the sea bottom deep enough to hold Mount Everest with seven Empire State Buildings piled on top, and then a very long ladder to reach the surface? Such a place exists in the western Pacific Ocean—the Philippine Trench is close to 11.5 kilometres (38 feet) deep and is believed to be the deepest part of this planet's oceans.

remote operated vehicle (ROV)

The strange-looking cirrate octopus lives at a depth of around 3,500 metres (11,500 feet) and is rarely seen alive.

white crabs

molluscs

Caring for the sea

Of all living things, we humans have developed the most marvellous piece of grey matter in the known universe—the human brain. With our extraordinary brains, we learned how to change the environment to suit our needs—the needs of an unnaturally large, and ever-increasing human population!

TAKING RESPONSIBILITY

Over time, humans have damaged the environment. We have hurt the sea through chemical pollution, high technology fishing, dynamite and cyanide fishing, and our preference for eating animals at the top of the food chains. If this behaviour continues, the damage may be permanent. We must take responsibility for our environment. Did you know that a southern blue fin tuna must eat about 17 kilograms (36 pounds) of pilchards to increase its weight by a mere 1 kilogram (2 pounds)? Perhaps it would be more sensible to eat more pilchards and less tuna. Yet good things are happening. These days, marine science education programs are run in many countries, and laws are in place to control ocean pollution.

stormwater outlet

Litter pollutes the sea and can be hazardous to wildlife.

About half of the world's coral reefs are in danger. Scientists consider that 10 per cent of reefs are damaged beyond repair.

If we look after our oceans, then we can continue to enjoy paddling in the shallows, building sand castles, wind-surfing and diving among the fishes.

Oil slicks are a great threat to sea life.

If people are unable to keep the oceans healthy, then maybe we will become extinct—just like the great dinosaurs!

LOOK
AGAIN!
The sea bird is also a victim of the oil spill from the container ship.

A crabby cleaner

Imagine a hermit crab picking up the rubbish at your school! Hermit crabs are very good at finding scraps of food. But be careful—they are sometimes known as 'robber crabs', so keep an eye on your lunch!

A DISTINCTIVE CRAB

Most crabs have a hard outer shell, but the hermit crab does not have this kind of protection. It must search the seabed for a disused shell to live in. And when it grows too big for its home, the hermit crab has to move to another shell. Would your school yard have somewhere suitable for the crab to live? The hermit crab has two pairs of walking legs so it can cover a lot of ground, and its strong pincer claws allow it to grasp its prey—or the remains of someone's sandwich!

Make an underwater viewer

Find a piece of plastic pipe or clay pipe about 35 centimetres (14 inches) long. Cover one end of the pipe with plastic food wrap or clear cellophane, holding it in place with string or an elastic band. Now gently put the covered end into a rock pool, being careful not to hurt any of the creatures living there, and take a look. What can you see?

Sometimes an anemone takes up residence on the outside of the hermit crab's shell, gathering scraps of food from around the crab's mouth. The crab doesn't mind, because the anemone's tentacles protect the crab from enemies.

CLASS 3B

GLOSSARY

aerated Full of dissolved air (and thus, oxygen).

algae Simple seaweed plants.

arthropod An animal with jointed legs and a skeleton on the outside of its body.

bivalve Mollusc animals with two external shells hinged together.

cnidarians (nee-DARE-ee-ans) The group of invertebrate animals, such as jellyfish and corals, with stinging tentacles around the mouth.

cockle A common bivalve.

crustaceans A large, varied group of arthropods found both in the sea and on shore.

detritus Decomposing parts of animals and plants.

ecdysis (ec-DIE-sis) The shedding of the outer covering of an animal's body.

environment The features of the place where an animal or plant lives and that influence the way it lives.

exoskeleton A skeleton covering the outside of an animal's body.

food chain A 'chain' of living things in which each living thing is thought of as a link in the chain. Each 'link' feeds upon the one below and is eaten by the one above.

habitat A place where an animal or plant lives.

hydrothermal vents Cracks in the Earth's crust where hot liquid or gas material enters the seabed.

iguana A tropical lizard with distinctive-shaped teeth.

intertidal The strip of shore-line between tidal high-water and low-water marks.

kelp Large brown seaweed.

limestone A rock or rock-like substance made of calcium carbonate.

mollusc A soft-bodied invertebrate often enclosed by one or more shells.

moult To shed the outer covering of an animal's body. Also, the cast-off covering.

nematocyst A tiny organ consisting of a capsule that contains a thread that can be

GLOSSARY

ejected, causing pain or death to prey animals.

octopod Another name for octopus.

photosynthesis The chemical process of building food materials using sunlight energy, carbon dioxide and water in the bodies of plants. During the process, oxygen gas is liberated.

phytoplankton Plankton that are plants.

pipi A small, smooth-shelled, burrowing bivalve.

plankton Animals and plants that float or drift in the sea.

polyp A small, soft-bodied animal with a body shaped like a column.

predator An animal that kills and eats other animals.

prey An animal killed and eaten by a **predator**.

pycnogonid The group of arthropods known as 'sea spiders' because of their resemblance to spiders. They are not true spiders.

salinity Referring to salty water and in particular the amount of dissolved sodium chloride present.

'smokers' Hydrothermal vents releasing lots of black, sulfurous gases and minerals.

spicules Barbed spheres embedded in the flesh of some sponges.

superheated steam Water hotter than its boiling point and containing no particles of moisture.

tsunami (soo-NAR-mee) A large (but not always high) fast-moving sea wave caused by an earthquake. Tsunamis are often catastrophic.

venomous Having glands capable of producing and releasing poisonous fluid.

vertebrate An animal with a spinal column and backbone constructed of vertebrae bones.

vomer teeth Teeth growing from the upper central roof bones of the mouth.

zooplankton Plankton that are animals.

zooxanthellae A group of tiny, single-celled **algae**.

FIND OUT MORE ABOUT UNDER THE SEA

BOOKS

Bennett, Isobel, *Australian Seashores*, WJ Dakin's Classic Study, Angus & Robertson, Sydney, 1987.

Coleman, Neville, *Encyclopedia of Marine Animals*, Angus & Robertson, Sydney, 1991.

Elder, D. L., and Pernetta, J. C., *Atlas of the Oceans*, Chancellor Press, Reed International Books, 1996.

Gould, Stephen (ed.), *The Book of Life*, Random House Australia, Sydney, 1993.

Greenaway, Theresa, Gunzi, Christiane, and Taylor, Barbara, *Ocean: The Living World*, Dorling Kindersley Ltd, London, 1994.

Lipson, Reg, *The Living Ocean*, Australia Post, 1998.

Norris, John, *Oceans: Nature Hide and Seek*, Hamlyn Children's Books, London, 1991.

Parker, Steve, *Fish, Eyewitness Guides*, Dorling Kindersley, London, 1997.

Paxton, J. R., and Eschmeyer, W. N. (eds), *Encyclopedia of Fishes*, University of New South Wales Press, Sydney, 1994.

Rudloe, Jack, *The Erotic Ocean, a Handbook for Beachcombers and Marine Naturalists*, EP Dutton Inc, New York, 1971.

Sowden, Craig, *Sharks*, Investigate series, Random House Australia, Sydney, 2000.

Steele, Philip, *Sharks and Other Monsters of the Deep*, Random Century Australia, Sydney, 1991.

Tuck, Lynne, *Whales*, Investigate series, Random House Australia, Sydney, 2000.

WEBSITE

Smithsonian Institute National Museum of Natural History

http://seawifs.gsfc.nasa.gov/ocean_planet.html

INDEX

INDEX

INDEX

INVESTIGATE

COLLECT THE SERIES

BEETLES **AUSTRALIA** **SPIDERS** **PLANES** **DINOSAURS**

 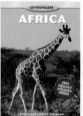   

BIG CATS **AFRICA** **ANTS** **SHARKS** **FROGS & TOADS**

   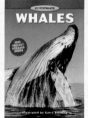 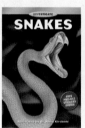

UNDER THE SEA **NORTH AMERICA** **RACING CARS** **WHALES** **SNAKES**

SHIPS & BOATS **SOUTH AMERICA** **SPACE**

Look out for these at your local bookseller